From Dad

How to Manage Your Money

How to Manage Your Money

Financial Strategies for Active Christians

From the Success in Christian Living series—a practical approach to achieving your goals for time, money, motivation, and human potential.

by Dennis E. Hensley

Published by Warner Press
Anderson, Indiana

All Scripture passages, unless otherwise indicated, are from the Holy Bible, King James Version ©1972 by Thomas Nelson, Revised Standard Version ©1972, by Thomas Nelson, or New International Version ©1987 by New York International Bible Society.

ISBN 0-87162-475-3

Printed in the United States of America
Warner Press, Inc.
Arlo F. Newell, Editor in Chief
Dan Harman, Book Editor
Caroline Smith, Editor

Contents

Page

Introduction vii

Part 1: Find a Level of Financial Contentment

1: Take Charge 3

2: A Hard Lesson 5

3: Basic Financial Planning 9

4: Cash Flow Management 13

Part 2: Determine Your Financial Circumstances

5: Get Out of Debt 21

6: Make Friends with the Budget 25

7: That Long-Range View 29

Part 3: Maximum Profits from Minimum Investments

8: The Smiths, the Wilsons, and Retiring with a Million 43

9: Perspiration Equity—By the of Your Brow 49

10: A Penny Saved 55

11: Profits from the Past 57

12: Know Book Value 59

13: Automatic Investments 61

Part 4: Get the Most for Your Money

14: Ways to Reduce Taxes 67

15: Varieties of Income 69

16: Use Social Security 71

17: Cover All Your Bases 73

Introduction: Stewardship and Vision

Many people have observed that the reason Jesus spoke so much about money matters is because, quite frankly, money **matters.** More than two thousand verses in the New Testament refer to money or material possessions, which is four times as many verses as those that relate to heaven and hell. Of Christ's thirty-eight parables, sixteen relate to various aspects of financial matters. In the Old Testament the Proverbs contain dozens of references to money and business; the other books are filled with episodes and incidents of how greed, ambition, and misuse of money led to tragic fates for many individuals. The taint of selling one's soul for thirty pieces of silver had its symbolic foreshadowing long before the crime of Judas. But does this mean that money is something sacrilegious? Definitely not!

Money, itself, is a wonderful thing. It can be used for many worthy pursuits. Joseph of Arimathaea was a wealthy man who used some of his money to pay for burial linen and a tomb for Jesus (Matthew 27:57-60). Zacchaeus was a rich man who gave half of all his possessions to the poor (Luke 19:8). King Solomon proclaimed money to be "a defense" (Ecclesiastes 7:12) that could "answereth all things" (Ecclesiastes 10:19). Money itself is not something evil.

Indeed, money is a very good thing. Nevertheless, when human beings allow their nature to lust after the hoarding and accumulating of money for the sake of self-aggrandizement, personal vanity, and opulent indulgences, they err. Money is not bad, but that all-consuming "love of money" (1 Timothy 6:10) truly is sinful.

But how does a Christian maintain righteous behavior concerning personal money management? How does stewardship (Luke 12:42) combine with faith in God's loving care for us? (See Matthew 6:31-32.) How does one balance a call to be a diligent laborer (2 Timothy 2:6) with an endorsement to be a discerning speculator, too (Matthew 25:21)?

The answer each time is to study the Scriptures in order to learn the foundational teachings of what the Bible has to say about money. For example, one continuous message throughout the Bible is that uncontrolled debt is wrong for a godly person. Knowing this, one can discern that speculating (investing) for one's personal gain is not proper conduct for a Christian unless he or she is properly meeting the repayment schedules of any agreed-upon debts.

The purpose of this book will be to present many, though not all, of the Bible's lessons about the proper use of money. Additionally, this book will show you how to manage your money in the most effective and responsible way. At the onset, I want to advise you to seek the help and advice of a trustworthy financial advisor—a CPA, CFP or MBA—whenever you are in need of extensive tax counseling or business planning recommendations. In the meantime, however, this book can serve to open your eyes to financial opportunities that you may not have been aware of previously.

It is proper for you to be a student of money management. J. Paul Getty, billionaire oil magnate, once said, "No man's opinions are better than his information." The Bible had already offered that advice three thousand years earlier when Proverbs 23:23 stated, "Buy the truth, and sell it not; also wisdom, and instruction, and understanding." As you read this book, you will find that same lesson taught over and over again: all wisdom related to money management has been available to us in the Bible for thousands of years. It simply falls to us to study it and then apply it.

—D.E.H.

Part 1:

Find a Level of Financial Contentment

You have many decisions to make in this life. The decisions you make about how to handle money, however, will have a profound impact on your life. Money can even have an impact on your relationship with Christ. Chapter 1 will illustrate how important it is to take responsibility for your finances.

Chapter 1:
Take Charge

For several years I have served as chairperson of the school board of a Christian elementary school. During years in which the school has been strong financially, our practice has been to award grants, scholarships, and tuition discounts to needy families. I recall one year, however, when our school was forced to enter the age of computer training. The cost of all the new electronic equipment drained our budget. No money was available for tuition discounts, and only those families with cash were allowed to enroll their children for the new academic year.

One man, the father of three children in our school and two younger children still at home, was amazed when his family's annual application for free tuition was denied. Angrily, he confronted me at church one Sunday morning and demanded to know what I was going to do to see that his children received a proper Christian education.

"What am I going to do about **your** children?" I responded. "Why, pray for them, of course, as I do for all the children in our school. But beyond that, nothing."

The man's face turned red. "How dare you drop my children from the school's roster! Don't you believe children should attend Christian schools?"

"Yes, I do," I said. "But it's expensive. That's why my wife and I limited our family to two children, so that we could afford to educate and rear them according to the limits of our budget. You and your wife chose to have five children. That was your choice and it's none of my business. What *is* my business, however, is running our Christian school in a fiscally sound way. And that takes money. So, brother, I want you to know that I love you and your family in the Lord, but if you can't pay the tuition fees I won't be admitting your three children to our school this year."

The matter did not end there. The man decided to go over my head. He made an appointment to see our pastor so that he could lodge a personal complaint against me. To the man's great shock, however, the pastor not only backed me in my decision, but he also took that opportunity to ask the man why he had not been faithful with his tithing and why he never contributed to offerings for mission work and church-sponsored charities.

The man's only defense was that he "couldn't afford" to give away any of the money he made. It took everything he earned to support a family of seven.

"If that's so," said the pastor, "why did you ever decide to have a family of seven?"

"Because I love children," the man countered.

"And I love cars," said the pastor. "But I don't have five cars in my driveway when I can only afford one. Large families provide many blessings, but they also present many constraints and limitations. It's time you learned that other Christians are not obligated to pay for the luxuries you desire in life. I'm afraid that educating your children at a Christian school is one 'luxury' you're not going to have for a while."

The pastor and I gave this man a few days to think about his situation. We then asked him to come and meet with us for a talk. When he arrived, we spent time in prayer and then counseled the man about proper stewardship. The man's anger melted and he began to get excited about opportunities to manage his money more effectively.

Things turned out well for this man and his family. By developing a strict budget, he controlled all loose spending of funds. The man and his wife signed up to work part time at the school as crossing guards, playground monitors, lunch room assistants, and school building custodians as barter for tuition discounts for their children. The oldest son in the family lined up a summer job and paid his own registration and book fees. Thanks to these measures and others, the three children were able to continue their education at our Christian day school.

Chapter 2:
A Hard Lesson

Because Christians are so used to singing songs about a heavenly Father who "owns the cattle on a thousand hills" and are so used to reading verses that admonish them to "lay up treasures in heaven," they sometimes begin to believe they have no personal responsibility to be good managers of money. Such beliefs usually lead to disaster, surprises, shocks, and confusion.

Consider these situations for a moment. Why do you suppose the Apostle Paul thanked the congregation at Philippi so graciously for the money the people sent him? (See Philippians 4:18.) Because that money enabled him to live and preach, that's why. Why do you think Joseph instructed the Egyptians to store so much grain during the prosperous years? (See Genesis 41:48). Because he knew the drought was coming and only the prudent people who prepared for lean times would survive, that's why.

Why did God the Father direct Wise Men to deliver gold and other gifts of wealth to the parents of the baby Jesus? Why did Christ curse the tree that failed to bring forth fruit? Why is the Old Testament so explicit in its laws about proper offerings?

We could ask questions similar to these for hours on end, and in each instance we would come back to the fact that God's people need to know the importance of financial management. "Do you see a man skillful in his work? he will stand before kings; he will not stand before obscure men." (Proverbs 22:29). The Bible states clearly that God gives us a great deal of personal freedom but that freedom carries with it equal opportunities to measure up to our responsibilities or slide to our lowest levels of failure.

Discovering that God expects us to be accountable for our actions is one of the most sobering moments in a Christian's personal maturity. It's a hard lesson and one that some of us have to be taught more than once before it sinks in.

Financial accountability is something all Christians must face. And the sooner, the better. If you stick your head in the sand and just hope that things will work out all right in the end, you'll discover "the end" will come a lot sooner than you had anticipated.

Look at the problem of inflation and how it secretly robs you. In 1952 and 1953 the inflation rate for 24 months was only 1.5 percent. As such, what cost you $10 to buy in 1951 climbed to $10.15 by the end of 1953. In 1979 and 1980, however, the inflation rate for 24 months was 25.7 percent. So, what cost you $10 in 1978 had skyrocketed to $12.57 by the end of 1980. Wow! That means that if you received a 5 percent raise in both 1979 and in 1980, you actually **lost** more than 15 percent of your money's buying power. Without understanding these factors, you might actually have thought that you were enjoying 10 percent more earning power.

Inflation is a zany rollercoaster. In 1972 it reached 12.2 percent, but by 1986 it was only 3 percent. A low inflation rate is not good news, though; it's just bad news to a lesser degree. I'll explain why. If inflation stays at a moderate 6 percent per year, every twelve years you will lose half of the purchasing power of whatever your money is now worth. That means that if you put one thousand dollars in a passbook savings account that earned you 5¼ percent per year, you would actually be **losing** buying power every year that you thought you were earning a profit. Now you know why we call times of tight money a depression. Thinking about it can depress anyone.

Since recessions, depressions, and eras of high inflation are realities of life in modern America, they should be confronted in pragmatic ways. You need to decide what sort of life you want to lead and then determine the amount of money you will need to pay for necessities and wants. Having reached a specific figure, it only remains to decide how you will obtain that money.

Naturally, the process is easier to follow in words than it is in actions. We know this because each year approximately 261,000 Americans file bankruptcy. Many thousands of others default on loans, have their purchased items repossessed, lose their credit status, and file for food stamps. People use money without understanding its tendency to get out of control. One financial counselor told me, "Too many people purchase things they don't actually need and charge them with cash they don't actually possess, in order to show off to folks they don't really like."

Whether you are guilty of that "status purchasing" syndrome or not, you probably can stand to run a check on your current uses of money. Let me touch on a few things worth thinking about:

The discipline of contentment—The Bible reminds us that we should have the spiritual and mental strength to be satisfied with what we have rather than dwell on what we lack. Paul wrote, "I have learned, in whatsoever state I am, therewith to be content" (Philippians 4:11). Sometimes if you will pause long enough to count your blessings, you'll discover that your cravings for unnecessary possessions will leave you.

The necessity to earn credit—Christ reminded us that people who prove their trustworthiness in small matters are soon given chances to prove their trustworthiness in larger matters. "He who is faithful in a very little is faithful also in much" (Luke 16:10). This certainly applies to cash management and credit ratings. If you want to be given a loan someday so that you can buy a five-bedroom home, make sure that you never miss a loan payment now on your two-bedroom home.

The responsibility to pay taxes—The Bible tells us that kings and rulers lead nations only with God's permission and, as such, the tribute we owe to our government should be paid ungrudgingly (Matthew 22:21).

The obligation to support the church—God admonished his people to bring all the tithes into the storehouse (Malachi 3:10), and to "honor the Lord with your substance" (Proverbs 3:9). It must never be forgotten that, although God owns everything, God is still honored when we return a portion to him of what he has given us. Tithes and offerings are tangible elements of worship and should be priority items in every Christian's budget.

Many Christians have offered a variety of views on money.

John Wesley advised the people of his day to "make all you can, save all you can, give all you can." Dr. Samuel Johnson wrote, "Men are seldom more innocently employed than when they are honestly making money." Henry Ward Beecher warned, "Debt rolls a man over and over, binding him hand and foot, and letting him hang on the metal fesh,* till the long-legged interest devours him." George MacDonald noted that, "But for money and the need of it, there would not be half the friendship in the world. It is powerful for good if divinely used. Give it plenty of air and it is as sweet as the hawthorn; shut it up and it cankers and breeds worms."

Secular philosophers have also offered a variety of opinions about money. Seneca the Roman said, "Money does all things for reward. Some are pious and honest as long as they thrive upon it, but if the devil himself gives better wages, they soon change their party." Benjamin Franklin taught, "If you would know the value of money, go and try to borrow some; for he that goes a-borrowing goes a-sorrowing." Tyron Edwards wrote, "To possess money is very well because it may be a most valuable servant; however, to be possessed by money is to be possessed by the meanest and worst kind of devil."

The range of these observations about money shows that money has potential for good or evil depending on how well it is handled. My favorite observation about money is by T. Starr King, who reminded us, "All our money has a moral stamp. It is coined over and over in the inward mint. The uses we put to it, the spirit in which we spend it, give it a character which is plainly perceptible to the eye of God." Realizing this, we are now ready to focus in the next chapter on a Christian strategy for money management.

*screen or sieve

Chapter 3: Basic Financial Planning

All financial planning, whether it be for a nation, a church, or just for your family unit, must begin with a basic understanding of the mathematical equation of sound economics. It reads like this:

Total Earnings		Accumulated Savings
+	=	+
Borrowed Cash		All Living Expenses

This formula is easy to understand. First you tally all your incoming cash *(Total Earnings)*, such as salaries, bonuses, gifts, overtime pay, garage-sale earnings, dividends, commissions, and inheritances already received. To this sum you add the total amount of all the money you have received in loans for your house, car, furnishings, appliances, vacations, college tuition, and investments *(Borrowed Cash)*. You now have a figure for the left side of the equation.

To figure the right side of the equation begin by adding up all of the money you have saved in CDs, savings accounts, checking accounts, bonds, stocks, investment notes, gold or silver coins, and real estate *(Accumulated Savings)*. Now add to this all the money you have to spend to meet the demands of your family budget *(All Living Expenses)*.

If both sides of the equation match, you are an excellent money manager. If the right side number is higher, then you are saving and spending money you've obtained on credit and this will doom you to eventual financial trouble. If the left side number is higher, you are either working too many hours and thereby are missing out on life or else you are borrowing so heavily you will soon find yourself overextended financially. To help us maintain the financial balance of this equation, we must understand six primary laws of cash flow management. That will be the topic of the next chapter.

Record of Living Expenses

	Amount Paid Monthly	Total Annual Amount
HOUSING		
Mortgage/Rent	______	______
Furnishings	______	______
Property taxes	______	______
Electricity	______	______
Heating	______	______
Water	______	______
Garbage Collection	______	______
Telephone	______	______
Yard work	______	______
Repairs/Maintenance	______	______
Remodeling	______	______
Neighborhood Assn. Dues	______	______
TOTAL	______	______

FOOD	________	________
CLOTHING	________	________
TRANSPORTATION		
License plates	________	________
Gas and oil	________	________
Maintenance/Repairs	________	________
Parking	________	________
New tires	________	________
TOTAL	========	========
ENTERTAINMENT/RECREATION		
Eating out	________	________
Babysitters	________	________
Periodical subscriptions	________	________
Vacations/Holidays	________	________
Clubs	________	________
Hobbies	________	________
TOTAL	========	========
MEDICAL EXPENSES		
Hospitalization Ins.	________	________
Physicians	________	________
Dentists	________	________
Optometrists	________	________
Pharmacists	________	________
TOTAL	========	========

INSURANCE		
Home	____	____
Life	____	____
Disability	____	____
Automobile	____	____
TOTAL	====	====
CHILDREN		
School lunches	____	____
Allowances	____	____
Tuition	____	____
Lessons	____	____
Club dues	____	____
Car pools/Bus fares	____	____
TOTAL	====	====
GIFTS		
Graduations	____	____
Christmas	____	____
Birthdays	____	____
Anniversary	____	____
Weddings	____	____
TOTAL	====	====
MISCELLANEOUS		
Tithe/Offering	____	____
Husband misc.	____	____
Wife misc.	____	____
Cleaning/Laundry	____	____
Pet care	____	____
Beauty/Barber	____	____
Garden	____	____
Jewelry	____	____
TOTAL	====	====
TOTAL LIVING EXPENSES	====	====

Chapter 4: The Laws of Cash Flow Management

If faithfully followed, the following six laws of cash flow management can revolutionize your finances.

Law #1: **Individuals must be aware of their personal finances.** You cannot say, "I have an accountant who keeps my books straight" or "My spouse handles our checkbook." What you don't know will surely hurt you. In her brutally honest book *Widow,* author Lynne Caine told of how she led a life of ease until her lawyer husband died. He left her no life insurance, no savings, and no investments. Worst of all, she had never had to live on a budget, balance a checkbook, or handle their taxes. As a result Mrs. Caine lost her home, her cars, her jewelry, her club memberships, and even most of her friends. Many years of hard work and dedicated study were required before she was able to get her life back on an even financial footing. Her husband had thought he was being a nice guy by not bothering his wife with all the burdens of paying bills and earning a living. His wife's ignorance about their financial affairs was devastating, however.

You should know how much your property is worth, what your level of debt is, and how much coverage you have in life, health, disability, home, car, and disaster insurance. You should understand your retirement plan and your current and future budget needs. Don't be in the dark about your personal finances. Ask questions; do some reading; check the numbers; help pay the bills; start keeping good records; examine receipts; talk about raises and deductions and taxes and savings. When it comes to your financial responsibilities, ignorance is not bliss; it is agony.

Law #2: **Individuals must set specific financial goals.** Spencer Johnson, co-author of *The One-Minute Manager,* stated recently that, "Goals are nothing more than dreams with a deadline." I like that because it applies so well to financial management. If you have a dream of one day owning a home and you take out a twenty-year mortgage to make the purchase, your dream has a deadline of twenty years in the future. If you have a dream of earning a college degree and paying back your loans for tuition within two years after graduation, you have a goal with a six-year deadline.

Nothing in the realm of financial success can be achieved without a goal. Financial success never "just happens"; nor is it ever obtained at the last minute.

The wonderful thing about setting a goal is that doing so will automatically present the necessary plan for achieving it. For example, if your goal is to retire early at age sixty with $500,000 in the bank, you then must work backward from age sixty to the age you now are to determine how much you will need to put into your retirement fund each year in order to accumulate $500,000. If you want to take a $7,000 vacation two years from now, that means you should try to save about $292 per month for the next twenty-four months.

Goal setting is especially important if your dreams are somewhat overwhelming. Suppose, for example, that your dream is "to get completely out of debt." That abstract statement will lead you to concrete procedures. If getting out of debt is your ultimate dream, you will need to find out what your total debt is (the target goal), where it stems from (bank loans, frivolous spending), and how to control it (cutting up credit cards, learning to ride in car pools). Step by step, you will close in on your target objective. You will be successful.

I would even encourage you to press yourself to a point beyond what you consider your maximum abilities to be. Don't put a ceiling on your potential. People are so afraid of not reaching a challenging goal that they set a small goal for themselves so that they won't feel like failures. That's too bad. I'd much rather come close to achieving a grand goal than actually achieve a minor goal.

When I became chairperson of that school board to which I referred earlier, we instituted an endowment fund for student scholarships. The board members suggested we set a goal of raising $25,000 in two years for this fund. I overruled their suggestion and changed the goal to $250,000—ten times higher than their original amount. We worked energetically for two years to meet that $250,000 goal. We weren't able to achieve it. We failed. We only raised $153,000. Nevertheless, we awarded a whole lot more scholarships to needy students thanks to that "failure" amount of $153,000 than we ever would have with a "successful" amount of $25,000. See the point? Okay, set your goals high.

Law #3: **Goals must be directed by budgets.** We observed before that setting a goal intuitively leads to forming plans to reach that goal. These plans must be financially in accordance with your cash-flow limitations. Creating a budget guards you from being blind-sided by an unexpected expense or a forgotten bill. It also serves as a tangible reminder that, **no,** you cannot **afford** to take out another loan or, **yes,** you do need to eat leftover spaghetti tonight rather than eat out at the local restaurant.

Budgets are constricting at first, but after a time they actually provide greater freedom. If your budget calls for you to set aside $10 per month for car maintenance, after a year you won't feel jolted financially if you suddenly need a new water pump or two new front tires or a new set of brakes. The money will be there.

Similarly, budgets can help build your confidence. Suppose you want to start saving money, but all you can afford is a mere ten dollars per week. On the one hand, that is a large amount of money to squeeze out of the total allowance for weekly expenditures; on the other hand, it sure doesn't look like much when you think of how little ten dollars will actually buy these days. It almost makes you not even want to try. By sticking to the budget for just one year, however, you will have $520. After the first week of the second year you can add another ten dollars. From this total of $530 you can take $525 to the bank and invest it in $1,050 of U.S. Savings Bonds. Follow the plan for five years and you will have $5,250 in bonds. It will give you a real feeling of security to cast your eyes on a stack of large denomination bonds all made out in your name.

Law #4: **Individuals should develop an investment strategy.** We mentioned before that it is your obligation to know your financial position in life. As you grow more comfortable in working with money and setting financial goals and developing budgets, you should continue to learn new things about money. You don't need to be a CPA in order to understand the basics of investments. Books, cassette recordings, and video tapes that explain about the stock market and other investment arenas can be borrowed from your public library. Time spent in study will literally be financially rewarding to you.

Let's go back to our example of the person who was going to save $292 per month for 24 months in order to take a $7,000 dream vacation. If that person, after the first year of saving, took the accumulated $3,504 and invested it in a one-year certificate of deposit paying 10 percent interest, it would provide more than $350 extra cash for the vacation.

Or what about our friend who could save only $10 per week? If that person knew how to set up a brokerage account, he or she could invest $100 every ten weeks and purchase a $1,000 zero-coupon bond. Then after five years, instead of having $1,050 in U.S. Savings Bonds, this person would have $26,000 in zero-coupon bonds. Hey!—now **that's** money, right?

But, to take advantage of all these extraordinary investment opportunities, you have to know how they work. That's where the time spent in study and in developing an investment strategy comes in.

Law #5: **Individuals must become disciplined financial managers.** To succeed in any field of endeavor a person must have discipline. This is particularly true in the area of financial management. Tightening the financial belt gets tedious and aggravating after a few months. It takes discipline not to grab the checkbook and go out and relieve the boredom by starting to spend again. It takes discipline to save money now for benefits in the future. It takes discipline to make payments on time in order to protect a credit rating.

Perhaps discipline is your hardest area to cope with. If so, you may have to put yourself into a position of **forced** discipline. People go about this many ways. Some people don't have enough discipline to save; so, they ask their employer to withdraw money for a payroll savings plan from their check before they ever get it. Some people turn their entire paycheck over to a financial counselor each week and then he or she pays the person's bills and gives whatever is left back to the individual. Some people have their paychecks mailed directly to their banks; after mortgage and other loan payments are deducted, the remaining balance is deposited into the individual's checking account.

Only through consistency does any financial plan succeed. We cannot achieve consistency without discipline. The discipline can be self-imposed, or it can be imposed on you, but it simply has to be there.

Law #6: **All financial actions should be God honoring.** If we begin with the premise that God owns everything, then our perspective on financial management will be one that makes us want to be good stewards of whatever God allows us to "tend" temporarily. Our tithes, offerings, and donations should be generous. Our business dealings should be honest. Our use of money should be purposeful rather than wanton. If we do this, we will hear our Lord speak as the person in Matthew 25:21 spoke: "Well done, good and faithful servant . . . enter into the joy of your master."

Summary

We have noted that we are personally responsible for our success or failure as money managers. We cannot be ignorant of money; nor can we expect other people to take care of us. Our decisions about how many children to have, how many loans to take out, and what careers to become involved in will all impact the way we live. These are personal choices and we have the freedom to choose whatever we wish. Our choices, however, also carry responsibilities and limitations and we must be mature in accepting these factors.

By following the six laws of financial management, we can maintain a grip on our money-related affairs. Learning them takes only a few minutes of reading; mastering them may take several years. Begin now.

Part 2: Determine Your Financial Circumstances

The first step in improving your financial situation is to determine where you currently stand.

What you have and what you owe are called your assets and your liabilities. Use the form titled "How Much Are You Worth?" to provide a total cash value of your accumulated material wealth. This amount may shock you or it may pleasantly surprise you, but either way it will inform you of what your actual asset values are.

Next you must determine the total amount of outstanding debts you are carrying. If you are not sure of your liabilities, take time to tally the remaining balances owed on your home, automobiles, credit cards, personal property loans, life insurance loans, business loans, stock leverage borrowings, and all private debts. To determine your **net worth,** subtract your total liabilities from your total assets. If you owe less than you own, you are solvent. If you owe more than you own, you are insolvent—or over your head in debt!

If you are solvent, your goal will be to increase your margin of solvency. That is, you will want to increase the value of your assets while you simultaneously are reducing your number of liabilities. Accomplishing this will increase your cash flow and raise your standard of living.

The form marked **Increasing Your Margin** will help you determine how to cut back on your outflow of cash expenditures so that "new" money can be made available to apply to existing debts. For example, under "Reduce Living Expenses" you might write in "cancel newspaper and magazine subscriptions for one year" and "disconnect cable TV for one year" and "cancel lawn care service for one year." These three items might equal $400. The money can be applied to some loan noted under "Reduce Debt By." This will reduce your debts by $400 and increase your assets by $400, so it will be an $800 margin improvement. Additionally, you will save interest costs by paying off your debt ahead of schedule; this will also increase your margin.

If, on the other hand, you are insolvent, you will need to use the form titled, **Strategy for Debt Reduction.** Rather than thinking about acquiring assets, your concentration will be solely on eliminating debt so that you can break even before you have your creditors foreclose on you.

In Part 2 we will look at ways to get out of debt, set up a budget, and do some long-range financial planning.

Chapter 5:

Get Out of Debt

Getting out of debt is much harder than getting into debt. It calls for some drastic measures. One pastor I know does a great deal of counseling with couples who have become buried in debt. This pastor refuses to work with people, however, unless they are sincerely committed to paying off their debts. To judge their sincerity, he puts them to a test: during their first session together he hands the husband and wife each a pair of scissors and orders them to remove all their credit cards and to cut them into pieces. If they refuse, the pastor refuses to continue the counseling.

Debt is not something that will go away if ignored. Just the opposite is true. By not repaying a debt, the interest on that amount compounds. Credit-card companies charge from 15 to 26 percent interest. Each month that you let your credit-card debt carry over to the next month, you greatly increase your total level of debt. The only way to control or reverse this costly process is by paying off the interest and the principle just as soon as possible.

Some people get so overwhelmed by debt that they don't know what to do. As a result, they take what little money they have and spend it on frivolous things in order to keep up appearances or convince themselves things really aren't so bad. This is both naive and dangerous.

If you really want to get out of debt, here's how:

1. Make a list of all your current debts and the percentage of interest you are paying on those debts.

2. Send a letter to all your creditors and tell them that you are in financial difficulty, but your intention is to repay all your debts. Explain the token amount you can pay on each debt each month and enclose a check for the first payment.

3. After the token payments are paid to each creditor, take the bulk of your remaining money and pay it against your smallest bill. Do this each payday until that smallest bill is paid off. Follow the same procedure for the next smallest bill and on up the line until all your debts are paid.

4. Add no new debts to your existing list of debt items.

You can perform a variety of helpful steps to help speed up the debt-reduction process. Wear last season's wardrobe rather than spend money on new clothes or seek out the second-hand thrift shops. If you have two cars, sell one and start to car pool or use public transportation. You'll save on gasoline, oil, maintenance, and insurance costs, and in addition you will have the cash you received for the auto sale.

Another idea is to hold a garage sale—a big one. Sell your extra stereo equipment, spare furniture stored in the basement, outgrown children's clothes, old toys, appliances you seldom use, books you've read, and jewelry you no longer wear. Apply your income from this sale directly to your debts.

Consider taking on another job. Perhaps you can baby-sit or do typing in your home or host Avon or Tupperware parties or log some overtime at the factory or do some extra sales work on Saturdays. Any extra income can be applied to the debt load.

Try to reduce spending by bartering. Some Christian day schools will provide a 50 percent tuition discount for students whose mothers will work two hours per day as playground supervisors, lunchroom helpers, librarians, or teachers' aides. The money budgeted but not spent for tuition can be applied to other debt.

Juggle your loans to reduce interest payments. If you have a personal loan of $10,000 on which you are paying 12 percent interest, you would be wise to borrow money from the cash value of your life insurance policies at a low rate of 3 to 8 percent and apply this money to the larger debt. If you borrowed $5,000 at 5 percent from an insurance policy and paid it against your personal loan, you would then owe $5,000 at 12 percent and $5,000 at 5 percent. That would **save** you 7 percent of interest on that second

$5,000. At compounded quarterly rates, that means you will save more than $370 in interest payments **per year.**

Weigh the idea of selling your home. If your monthly mortgage-tax-insurance payment is too heavy a burden, you may have moved into your dream home before you were ready for it. If so, sell it and rent an apartment or move into a smaller, more reasonably priced home.

Continue to think about ways to generate money that can be applied to your debt. Every dollar applied to the principle owed on an outstanding loan will reduce both the debt load **and** the amount of future interest you will have to pay on that loan. That sort of progress will be very encouraging to you.

The next chapter contains tips on making a spending plan that will greatly improve your financial circumstances.

Strategy for Debt Repayment

In the following columns, list all of your current creditors according to those with the highest rates of interest down to those with the lowest rates. Make a commitment to pay a set amount to each creditor each month. List that monthly amount and then list the pay-off date (your goal). Send a letter to each of these creditors and explain your intentions. Should you receive any unexpected extra money, apply it to the bill costing you the most in interest.

	Creditor	Balance Owed	Interest Rate	Amount Per Month	Pay-Off Date
1.	________	________	________	________	________
2.	________	________	________	________	________
3.	________	________	________	________	________
4.	________	________	________	________	________
5.	________	________	________	________	________
6.	________	________	________	________	________
7.	________	________	________	________	________
8.	________	________	________	________	________
Totals		________		________	

Intended Future Purchases

As an incentive for you to pay off your debts as soon as possible, make a list of some of the things you plan to buy once you are debt-free (such as new furniture, a VCR, a set of encyclopedias):

Item	Amount

Chapter 6: Make Friends with the Budget

In the previous chapter we emphasized tried and true ways for getting out of debt. In this chapter you will find information for setting up a workable spending plan. The chart "Personal Monthly Budget" is a simple model for setting up your plan. It contains two columns. In the first column you can list the amount of cash you are presently spending on each of these line items. In the second column put down dollar amounts that would modify some of your present expenditures.

Certain categories, such as mortgage payments, insurance premiums, tithe, and taxes cannot be altered much without major changes in your life-style. Other categories, however, can be modified substantially if you will agree to discipline yourself more. These areas include money allotted for clothing, housecleaning services, gifts, magazines, books, sports, membership dues, boat care, motorcycle care, and vacations.

In households with one responsible adult, that person will assume responsibility for putting the budget to work. When husband and wife make up the household, the best way to make effective use of a budget is by working together with it. Here are some suggestions for this:

1. **Designate responsibilities:** Assign responsibilities for such areas as groceries, utilities, medical care, mortgage payments, car maintenance, and lawn care. Divide the list of bills and insist that each spouse live within the budgeted amount listed for each line item.
2. **Compare monthly results:** Examine the receipts and cancelled

checks to insure that last month's budget was met before you spend money on this month's budget.

3. Save unspent balances: If money is left over after all the budgeted expenses have been covered, put that money into savings or apply it directly to the principle of your mortgage or another outstanding debt.

4. Cope with emergencies: If a large unexpected bill comes up, do not let it threaten your budget. Either pay the bill with your savings or pay it with money from another line item (one less urgent) that you can repay to yourself later. It is much better to be in debt to yourself than to someone else!

Many times when people first look at their budgets, they believe there are no items that can be trimmed or eliminated. But is that really true? Back during the Arab oil embargo of 1978, Americans learned how to turn thermostats down to 68 degrees. They saved gas by forming car pools and using push lawnmowers. They used candles and barbecue grills for light sources and cooking. They read books instead of turning on radios and televisions. The point is that we can reduce our spending levels in many ways if we really put our minds to the task **and** are committed to succeeding.

Many people will insist that budgets won't work because of the constant number of unbudgeted "necessities." For example, the cost of holidays can add many hundreds of dollars to a budget if not kept under control. These expenses can be handled in creative ways, however. Let me share a few ideas with you:

Anniversaries and Valentine's Day: Give your loved one a handwritten book of coupons, each redeemable upon request. The coupons can be for such services as washing the dishes, cleaning the garage, waxing the car, cutting the lawn, washing windows, bathing the dog, giving a backrub before bed, or fixing a favorite meal.

Christmas and Birthdays: Gifts that are made by hand are usually only 25 percent as expensive as purchased gifts. Sometimes a gift can be pragmatic. A nice gift for a son or daughter going away to college could be a laundry bag filled with washing powders, fabric softener, bleach, and a roll of quarters for the laundromat. A gift for dad could be an inexpensive plastic box with emergency things for the car, such as maps, spare fuses, a small flashlight, an ice scraper, a roll of electrical tape, a flare, and a pair of cloth work gloves.

Easter and Thanksgiving: Pitch-in dinners with friends can provide times of warmth and fellowship while also spreading the meal costs over two or three families. Plan a time after the meal for devotions, reading of poems, watching home movies, playing board games, and visiting.

Another thing that seems traditional in American culture, yet can be a budget wrecker, is the family vacation. We all seem to feel that after a year of hard work we **deserve** a relaxing and fun-filled week or two of frivolity. The problem is that by the time we pay for air fare, hotels, meals, tips, car rental, admission fees, and souvenirs, we can easily have paid out more than $1,500. Besides that, the "vacation" can leave us feeling exhausted. If we charge it to a credit card, that will add another $350 per year in interest payments. A week or two of summer fun can set back our entire hope of ever recovering from previous financial disasters. Instead, we must use vacation days in more practical ways. Here are ideas:

- Picnics at the park
- Visits to area museums and art galleries
- Family work days around the house enlivened with homemade treats for all the helpers
- Block parties and neighborhood cookouts
- Pajama parties, sleepovers, and visits from relatives
- Participation in vacation church school, Little League, day camp, and sports clinics
- Hikes at a wildlife reserve
- Summer reading programs at the public library
- Planting and tending a garden
- Bicycle rodeos
- Take part in a civic drama production
- Attend free outdoor fireworks displays, band concerts, county fairs, city parades, and flower shows
- Take a free tour of area factories, offices, and businesses
- Organize a scavenger hunt
- Form a neighborhood aerobics club
- Do canvassing work for your church
- Create a backyard carnival to raise funds for a charity

- Invite a visiting missionary to live in your home for a week
- Tour a zoo
- Do odd jobs for extra income

Whereas visiting Hawaii or going camping in northern Canada may be an exotic way to spend your vacation days, dozens of other fun activities can be enjoyed that will be free or of minimal cost. Be creative in your thinking and planning and you will not have to destroy your established budget.

Let me add a few final words of insight on budgets. If you find that after using a budget for two or three months you are somehow still coming up short of cash, put a small notebook in your pocket and make a note of every item you spend money on. What you will discover is that you are doing a lot of unnoticed spending. If you put 50 cents per day into a soda pop machine, toss in a dollar or two each week for collections taken at the office, buy an occasional newspaper, pack of gum, ink pen, or magazine, all this will add up to an invisible five or ten dollars of money spent each week. That can lead to 40 or 50 dollars vanishing from your monthly budget. You will either have to stop all extra spending or else revise the distribution amounts in your budget.

Similarly, if the budget makes you feel like a prisoner who is serving a long, drawn-out sentence, keep a chart or graph of your monthly debt reduction progress. As you see that graph line go down, down, down, drawing closer and closer to the zero debt level, you'll be encouraged to gut it out a while longer. Most people can endure just about anything as long as they know for sure that a definite end to their misery is in sight.

Finally, once you have used your budget to control your spending and eliminate your debt, continue to use it even when good times return. Just as you slowly yet steadily dug yourself out from your burden of debt, you can just as steadily begin to build a portfolio of sound investments and savings. If, for example, your budget allowed you to pay 250 dollars per month against existing debts, that money can now be put into a savings account, U.S. savings bonds, CDs, stocks, or other securities. In this manner your budget will not only keep you out of debt, but it actually will make it possible for you to pay cash for your future purchases. Now that's progress!

Chapter 7:
That Long-Range View

In determining your financial circumstances, you must not be nearsighted. Some people believe that they are in solid financial shape because they are earning each month exactly the amount of money they are spending. Economists call this "living up to one's income." For a time, this system will work well; sometimes young couples with two incomes can go along this way for five or ten years and never feel any financial constraints or pressures. Nevertheless, it can't go on forever. And when change comes, it really comes in a major way.

Let's consider the case of Irving and Charlene. This happy couple married after college, bought a nice home, furnished it beautifully, purchased two new cars, and even hired a housecleaner to come in twice each week to keep up the house. This standard of living was high for newlyweds, but Irving was earning good commissions at his insurance job, and Charlene was earning a good salary and benefits package teaching third grade. To them, it was logical to spend $27,000 annually for the good life because that was what they were earning.

This happy scenario continued for five years. No installment payments were ever missed, but neither was any money put aside for savings and investments. Then Charlene became pregnant. Her baby was due to be born in October. Thus she took a year's leave of absence after finishing the current school year. That autumn Irving and Charlene found themselves in financial difficulty. They no longer had Charlene's salary. They suddenly had a new baby to feed, clothe, and care for. And they were handed new bills for the baby's delivery.

The situation then got worse. Irving stayed home some evenings to care for the new baby while Charlene caught up on her rest. This prevented Irving from visiting insurance clients during the evenings and, as a result, his level of commissions started to drop drastically. Furthermore, since Charlene was no longer on salary at her school, she was notified that she would have to pay for her own retirement benefits, hospitalization insurance, association dues, and other benefits if she wanted them to continue during her leave of absence.

Things started to change greatly at this household. They discontinued use of the housecleaning service. One of their two cars was sold. Spending for nonessential items was halted. Still, it wasn't enough. Christmas shopping and year-end taxes came due just six weeks after the baby was born. Irving began again to use a credit card, telling himself that he would pay everything off later when Charlene went back to work.

But Irving never did catch up. Charlene preferred to stay home with their baby for two years. Even then, the couple had to pay for full-time care of their child. Charlene's return to her profession necessitated purchase of a second car and a new wardrobe. Bills, carry-over debt, and compounding interest were increasing faster than the new influx of cash flow. Ultimately, Irving and Charlene had to sell their house and many of their furniture items and move into an economically priced apartment. By that time, Charlene was pregnant with their second child and ready to take another leave of absence from work the following year.

As you see, today's prosperity does not insure tomorrow's prosperity. Thus, to determine your financial circumstances you must project your thinking and planning several years into the future. You must ask yourself serious questions and prepare now for the solutions and answers. Begin by considering such basics as those in these circumstances:

1. If your aged parents need nursing home care, who will pay for it?

2. If you or your spouse become disabled, how will you earn a living?

3. If your children want to attend college, how will you pay for it?
4. If you or your spouse dies, how will funeral costs be paid and where will the money come from for baby-sitters, repairs, and other people to do the work of the deceased spouse?
5. If you get fired or laid off, how will you survive while you are seeking a new job?
6. When it comes time for you to retire, how will you support yourself?

As you consider these questions, you will realize that the time to start planning for their solutions is now. This will cause you to review the way your current financial circumstances can be adjusted so that they exert a positive influence on your future financial circumstances. To help you in this, read and use the charts found in this chapter called "Life Insurance Record Sheet" and "Individual Retirement Accounts."

Charles Kettering once wrote, "The reason I think so much about the future is because that's where I expect to spend the rest of my life." This should also be true of you. Always remember that today's financial decisions will have a direct impact on tomorrow's financial circumstances. So, think ahead, plan, and be prepared.

How Much Are You Worth?

Current value of your home	________
Current value of other real estate (cottage, office buildings, or others)	________
Money owed to you	________
Life insurance cash value	________
IRAs, retirement pensions	________
Cash in your savings account	________
Mutual funds/stocks	________
Bonds	________
Works of art, collectibles (such as coins, stamps, antiques)	________
Furs, jewelry, gold, silver	________
Cash on hand	________
Checking account balance	________
Book value of your auto(s)	________
Home furnishings	________
Personal items (such as musical instruments, bicycles)	________
Outdoor items (such as tools, boat, lawn mower)	________
Goods in storage	________
Partnerships, venture capital	________
Others	________
	________
	________
	________
	________
	________
GRAND TOTAL	________

Increasing Your Margin

	Monthly Amount	Annual Amount
1. Reduce Living Expenses By:		
2. Reduce Debt By:		
3. Reduce Taxes By:		
4. Restructure Investments By:		

Total Margin Increase ________

Your Life Insurance Record Sheet

Company	Agent's Name	Issue Date	Policy Number	Type of Policy	Insured	Owner

Individual Policies:

Retirement Plan Policies:

Business Policies:

Mortgage Policies:

Beneficiary	Option for Waiver of Premium	Face Value	Cash Value	Cash Value Borrowed	Loan Interest Rate	Annual Premiums

Personal Monthly Budget

Regular Monthly Expenditures

Monthly Payments	Present	Modified
Rent or Mortgage Payments	$______	$______
Car Payments	______	______
Boat/Mobile Home/Motorcycle	______	______
TV/Appliance Payments	______	______
IRA Deposits	______	______
Repayment of Loans	______	______
Medical/Dental Plan	______	______
Life Insurance Premiums	______	______
Other Insurance Premiums (auto, home, cottage)	______	______
Miscellaneous Regular Payments (such as credit cards)	______	______
TOTAL	$______	$______

Household Operating Expenses

	Present	Modified
Telephone	$______	$______
Gas & Electricity	______	______
Garbage Collection	______	______
Water	______	______
Sewer Charges	______	______
Lawn Care	______	______
New Home Fixtures, Furniture	______	______
Repairs, Maintenance, Replacements	______	______
Other Household Expenses	______	______
TOTAL	$______	$______

Personal Living Expenses (for family)

Clothing (purchasing, cleaning, repair)	$_____	$_____
Doctor and Dentist Bills (not covered by insurance)	_____	_____
Education/Music Lessons/Tutors	_____	_____
Membership Dues	_____	_____
Maid Service/Baby-sitters	_____	_____
Gifts & Contributions	_____	_____
Auto Maintenance, Gas, Parking Fees	_____	_____
Travel/Vacations	_____	_____
Food (home and away)	_____	_____
Tithes/Church Offerings	_____	_____
Books, Newspapers, Magazines	_____	_____
Spending Money, Allowances	_____	_____
Entertainment/Sports/Fitness Clubs	_____	_____
TOTAL	$_____	$_____

Taxes

Federal, State, City Income Taxes	$_____	$_____
Property Taxes	_____	_____
Other Taxes	_____	_____
TOTAL	$_____	$_____

TOTAL: Monthly Payments, Personal Living Expenses, Household Operating Expenses, Taxes	$_____	$_____

Individual Retirement Accounts

The 1986 Tax Reform Act made sweeping changes in the laws regulating Individual Retirement Accounts (IRAs). Of the 40 million Americans who were investing regularly in IRAs, nearly 15 million were no longer eligible and another 7-½ million will be eligible only for a partial deduction. Here are the new guidelines:

For persons with no retirement plans:

A. Unmarried individuals can make tax deductible contributions to an IRA up to $2,000 annually, no matter how high one's earnings are.

B. If an employed person is married and her or his spouse is also employed, but neither is covered by a qualified retirement plan, both spouses can make up to $2,000 in annual tax deductible IRA contributions no matter how high their individual or joint earnings are.

C. If an employed married person has a spouse who is unemployed, the married worker can make annual tax deductible contributions up to $2,000 to his or her personal IRA and up to $250 to a spousal IRA.

For persons with qualified retirement plans:

A. Unmarried individuals with qualified retirement plans can deduct $2,000 annually for contributions to an IRA if they earn less than $25,000 annually. Between earnings of $25,000 through $35,000 deductions are reduced according to one's adjusted gross income. Beyond $35,000 no deductions are permitted.

B. If either spouse in a marriage is covered by a qualified retirement plan and the couple files a joint return, no tax deductions may be taken for contributions to an IRA if the couple earns more than $50,000 of adjusted gross income. The full $4,000 for a working couple or $2,250 for a couple with one working spouse may be deducted if the combined earnings (AGI) are under $40,000. If the combined income is between $40,000 and $50,000 of AGI, the $2,000 deduction is reduced by $200 for every $1,000 of income.

Summary

In Part 2 we learned how to take a cold and honest look at our current financial status, and we learned ways to determine how, when, and why we came to be where we are. This knowledge then gave us the perspective we needed to total up our assets and liabilities and to discipline ourselves through the use of a budget to increase the assets and reduce the liabilities. We further learned a variety of ways to help us stay loyal to the budget and not to lose faith in it. Finally, we learned how to look long range in our planning so that we wouldn't be caught off guard by major financial strains due in the future.

Christian stewardship begins by getting our own house in order. This often requires self-denial, strict discipline, careful planning, and strong faith. The rewards of peace of mind and a balanced life make it all worthwhile and reduce the liabilities. We further learned a variety of ways to help us stay loyal to the budget and not to lose faith in it. Finally, we learned how to look long range in our planning so that we wouldn't be caught off guard by major financial strains due in the future.

Christian stewardship begins by getting our own house in order. This often requires self-denial, strict discipline, careful planning, and strong faith. The rewards of peace of mind and a balanced life make it all worthwhile.

Part 3: Maximum Profits from Minimum Investments

Some wit has quipped that most Americans are so busy earning a living that they never make any money. Actually, that lament isn't anything new. More than twenty-five hundred years ago, the Bible noted, "You have sown much, and harvested little; you eat, but you never have enough; you drink, but you never have your fill; you clothe yourselves, but no one is warm; and he who earns wages earns wages to put them into a bag with holes (Haggai 1:6).

As a consumer-oriented people, we understand all too well the concept that our pockets, purses, and wallets have holes in them. We always intend to start saving and investing as soon as we "can afford to," yet that day never seems to arrive. When we look at our lives from a long-range perspective, we often scratch our heads and wonder where all the money went. **Why** wasn't **any** extra money ever available to save or invest?

The answer to that question is rooted in the consumption practices of most Americans. That will be the topic of the next chapter.

"Getting started saving is usually the hardest part . . . You cannot find a better time to start your investing than today."

Chapter 8:
The Smiths, the Wilsons, and Retiring with a Million

Americans vary widely in the manner in which they spend their money. Let me give you an example of a fictitious couple named Jean and Joe Smith. The Smiths have been married for fifteen years. They have a nice home, a three-year-old car, some lovely household furnishings, and two healthy children ages nine and thirteen. Recently, Joe Smith's employer had to lay off several employees because the company profits were low. Joe lost his job as a machinist, but after six months of government-sponsored career training he found a new job as a computer operator.

Joe was unemployed for six months. Now, his new job pays him ten thousand dollars less per year than his former job did because he's back to a first-year level of experience. As such, even though Joe is now working full time again, he and Jean find that they are in serious financial trouble. They cannot register their children for private school this fall because they still owe four months unpaid tuition from last year. Their credit-card companies have canceled their charging privileges because they have run their bills to the limit and have not paid the interest rates due each month. Jean has had to drop out of two clubs because she can't pay the dues, and Joe has not been able to renew the subscriptions to his four favorite sports magazines because his checking account is flat.

One night Jean and Joe sat down at the kitchen table and looked at a stack of overdue bills, and invoices they had received. They were amazed that they could be in such drastic financial straits.

"I received a 10 percent raise every year for the past decade," said Joe. "Every year I made more money, yet we never saved a nickel. How could that be? If we just would have had a few thousand dollars put aside, we could have survived those six months when I was only drawing unemployment compensation. Now, we may lose our house and car to our creditors."

Interestingly enough, next door to the Smiths the Wilson family lived. Ron Wilson had worked side by side with Joe Smith for the fifteen years that they had both been employed as machinists. Ron was laid off when Joe was, and Ron, too, became employed as a computer operator six months later. Unlike the Smiths, however, the Wilsons did not end up in financial trouble.

Ten years earlier, Ron Wilson had signed up for the payroll savings plan at work. A small portion of his salary was withdrawn each payday and was used to purchase a government savings bond. Since the money was withdrawn and invested before it ever reached Ron's payroll envelope, he and his wife Sue never really missed it. Although each weekly investment was small, it mounted up with time. When Ron lost his job, his bonds were valued at $16,000. Needless to say, this monetary cushion was of great help to the Wilsons during the six months Ron was drawing unemployment compensation.

Another item that helped the Wilsons was a stamp collection. Sue Wilson and her two daughters had started collecting United States postage stamps in albums when the girls were young. It was an inexpensive and enjoyable hobby. Each month the girls would spend a few dollars to buy new issues of commemorative stamps. They would catalog and mount the stamps in their collector's books. The purpose of the collection was simply the enjoyment the girls received from seeing the many different styles and designs of stamps; they also learned a great deal about United States history by looking up information about the person or place the stamp was honoring.

When Ron lost his job, the Wilson girls were teen-agers. They were involved in the school orchestra, the young people's group at church, and in a variety of other activities. They no longer had as great an interest in stamp collecting as they had had previously. Sue Wilson knew the girls wanted to stay enrolled in the private

Christian school they were attending. To help pay the tuition, she suggested they sell the stamp collection to a local dealer. The girls readily agreed. To their surprise and joy, they discovered that their collection was worth $3,700 hundred dollars because of the variety and excellent condition of their stamps. The girls were able to stay in the school of their choice.

The difference between the tragedy of the Smith family and the stability of the Wilson family was that the Wilsons had realized early in life that even a little bit of saving and investing could make a major difference in a family's standard of living. The key factor, however, was that the saving had to come **first** and the rest of the family spending **second.** The Smiths had never learned this. Thus, when Joe received a raise, he bought a VCR, microwave oven, and other consumer goods and raised his standard of living to comply with his new level of cash flow. Joe and Jean became used to these "necessities." When the old ones wore out, newer (more expensive) ones were purchased to replace them. Actually, Joe's raises were spent before he ever brought them home. Nothing was left to save and invest. Joe became an example of the Bible's description of the person who earns wages to put into a bag with holes.

Perhaps you have been waiting for an inheritance or a major windfall before you begin to save and invest. If so, you are wasting valuable time during which your money could be increasing (and perhaps also providing you with an enjoyable hobby).

The compounding effect of small amounts of money is often amazing to people. For example, if you can double $1,000 on itself just ten times, you will have more than $1.1 million. If you start with just one penny and double it on itself for thirty-five consecutive days, you'll have more than $339 million.

Getting started saving is usually the hardest part. The longer time you have for your money to be invested, the richer you will become. You cannot find a better time to start your investing than today. Sometimes the results will be breathtaking. Let me tell you a couple of true stories to prove this to you.

Back in 1985 interest rates were still in the double digits. As such, it was possible to purchase United States treasury zero-coupon bonds for as low as $50 per thousand. This meant that if you paid $50 for a treasury zero bond in 1985 and held it for twenty-eight years, it would be worth a redeemable value of $1,000. It so happened that my brother, an accountant, was approached for advice from a nineteen-year-old client who had been in a serious car accident in 1985. She had received $20,000 as a lump-sum settlement for injuries she had sustained. The young woman wanted to invest the entire amount for her security later in life. My brother helped her invest it all in United States treasury zero coupon bonds. As a result, at the age of 47 in the year 2013, that woman will be able to redeem her $20,000 investment for **one million dollars.** Amazing, eh? Here's another story:

In 1987 a twenty-two-year-old man was honorably discharged from the army. He had saved some money during his enlistment, and so he invested $2,000 in a tax-deferred Individual Retirement Account (IRS). Since $2,000 is not a fortune, he asked this question of his broker: "If I continue to earn 12 percent interest each year on my initial investment of $2,000, how much more should I invest each year after that if I want to retire with a million dollars?" The broker gave a surprising answer. "If you invest $2,000 a year in an IRA for only six years, ages 22 to 27, and then never put another penny into your IRA, at age 65 it will be worth $1,348,440 if you continue to earn 12 percent each year. If you invested $2,000 each year from ages 22 to 65 at 12 percent, you would retire with $2,421,620, and you wouldn't have to pay any tax on that money until you started to withdraw it. Additionally, you would get a $2,000 tax deduction for each year that you made a maximum contribution."

These stories are absolutely stunning, aren't they? I have shared them with you as a way of proving that you can earn maximum profits from minimum investments. Never say, What I have to save and invest is so small that it won't make any difference anyway. Oh, yes, it will!

Later I am going to tell you the true stories of four people who earned huge profits with minimal investments and had a great deal of enjoyment while doing so. Their approaches were completely different yet equally successful. Reading about them will inspire you as well as get you to thinking about how you, too, can become a low-cost investor. Before we read about these people, however, we first need to discover the secret factor that led to their success:

it's something called **perspiration equity.** That will be the topic of the next chapter.

"You can start investing
with whatever
money you have
available."

Chapter 9:
Perspiration Equity—By the Sweat of Your Brow

"A little money invested wisely can lead to extraordinary returns if the investor also puts in some **perspiration equity,**" says Christian investments counselor Steve Summers. "Show me someone who is willing to do some reading and a bit of work and I'll show you someone capable of greatly multiplying his or her financial holdings."

Summers knows what he's talking about. In 1979 he left a low-paying teaching job and began training to become a broker and insurance agent. With a borrowed $10,000 he formed the H-S-S Real Estate Partnership, which now owns rental properties in Indiana, and the Summers Agency, a financial counseling service based in Fort Wayne.

Today, Summers lives in a sprawling home on two acres of land. He has a fully computerized office in the city. He owns two cars and he sends his daughters to private schools. Steve also serves as chairperson of his church's board, and he's active in a variety of civic and professional groups.

Equally important, however, Summers is showing his clients how they, too, can enhance their financial holding—even when they have very little capital with which to begin.

"The first step to do is to become knowledgeable about the type of investments into which you want to put your money," advises Summers. "The next step is to commit a certain amount of your time and energy (perspiration equity) toward making your investments prosper."

The investments to which Summers is referring are common

and easily accessible items, such as coins, antiques, books, stamps, records, autographs, baseball cards, undeveloped plots of land, metals, bonds, art, stock, or rental property. Anything that has an appreciable value to it—whether it is a ten-cent new issue stamp, a $10 first edition novel, or a $10,000 tract of industrially zoned land—can form the foundation of an investments portfolio.

"The mistake people make is in not getting started," admonishes Summers. "You don't need a fortune in order to begin. A little can become a lot, and the sooner you start, the better."

Summers specializes in helping people find the kinds of investments that fit their pocketbooks yet excite their imagination. He has helped many newlyweds set up investment programs that have led to new home purchases, and he has enabled them to fulfill their dreams of traveling and enjoying the good life.

"You are never too young or too old to begin an investments program," insists Summers. "Too many people feel they need to save a few thousand dollars before they can begin to invest. Most never put that much aside, and so they never develop **any** kind of investment program at all. Meanwhile, a newspaper carrier who only buys one United States savings bond per month manages to save $300 per year. In a few years when she or he redeems those bonds, their value has doubled to $600. The point is that you can start investing with whatever amount of money you have available.

Summers points out that most people are so impatient to enjoy life's pleasures that they spend all their income and never invest for the future.

"I knew of two young brothers who inherited about $900 each," recalls Summers. "One brother bought a pony and the other bought a calf. Each year one brother earned ribbons and awards at the 4-H Fair for his well-groomed and well-trained horse. The other brother put his grown steer on display, sold it, and used the money to buy three new calves. He raised them, sold them, and then bought nine calves, then twenty-seven calves, and so it went. When the boys finished high school, one had a horse that was too old to ride anymore. The other had a herd of nearly two hundred cattle that when sold not only paid for his college costs but a nice car as well. One had a vision of the future and the other didn't."

Summers suggests following a simple four-point plan when starting to invest:

1. Explore a variety of investments. Go to the magazine section of the public library and examine the investment, craft, and money-management magazines. Make a list of several investments that have a track record of increasing in value with time. Choose one that interests you and fits within your investment price range. Read as many books and articles about that investment as you can find.

2. Find mentors to guide you. In order to enhance your skills and knowledge about your specific investment, seek out people who can teach and coach you. Join clubs in which fellow enthusiasts can offer you their advice and experience. Develop a pen pal correspondence with traders and dealers across the country. Attend seminars, lectures, and trade fairs related to your investment.

3. Constantly upgrade your holdings. Begin to build your portfolio by buying whatever you can afford. Later, you can improve your holdings by trading what you have (and a little cash) for better quality pieces or more valuable investments. Buy extra quantities whenever you find a bargain. Learn how to trade, barter, negotiate, purchase, and sell.

4. Enjoy your investments. Keep in mind that investments are not only profitable, but also enjoyable. Hang your collection of paintings for people to see. Read the books you've collected. Talk with your children about your stamp collection. Wear your handmade lace shawls; display your antiques in your den.

"There's an old adage that says, 'Money begets money, and more money begets more money,' " says Steve Summers. "You don't need a fortune to begin an investment program; you just need the determination to get started."

Summers is right. You may be saying to yourself, "But what can I do? I have less than $500 to invest. Are any opportunities open to me?"

For a fact, you can take several steps. Here are a few examples:.

• **MMMFs.** In order to keep your money accessible yet allow it to earn more than a mere 5¼ percent interest in a savings account, you can join a money market mutual fund. Your money actually buys shares in the mutual fund. Your money is added to the cash put in by the other investors and then it is used to buy various bonds, securities, and stocks. As the fund prospers, the profits will be divided among you and the other investors. The rate of return is usually between 6 percent and 17 percent and you can spend your profits or reinvest them.

• **CDs.** For as little as $500, you can put your money into a certificate of deposit and earn a higher yield than a regular savings account. Bank CDs are issued for specific dollar amounts and pay a guaranteed interest rate over a specific period of time. A penalty is accessed for money that is withdrawn prior to the maturity date. Even IRA funds can be used to purchase IRA CDs, thus greatly increasing retirement fund earnings.

• **Gold Coins.** For longevity of growth and dollar strength, you cannot go wrong with gold bullion coins such as the Canadian maple leaf or the United States $20 gold piece. In 1970 gold was valued at $35 per ounce. In 1985 it averaged $350 per ounce (a 1,000 percent increase in just fifteen years). In 1987 it averaged $400 per ounce. During times of high interest rates, such as 1979, the price of gold has risen to $825 per ounce. To learn more about the market, contact the American Numismatic Association (ANA) at 818 North Cascade Avenue, Colorado Springs, Colorado 80903 or subscribe to *Coin World*, P.O. Box 150, Sidney, Ohio 45367.

• **Sharebuilder Plans.** For only $50 per month individuals can take part in Merrill Lynch's Sharebuilder Plan. The firm provides a list of suggested stocks that it sells at a 40 percent discount on commission. The investor selects the stock she or he wants and the firm purchases shares (or fractions of shares) for that person's portfolio. This allows even the small investor to become an owner of blue chip stocks. It's a perfect investment situation because if the price of the stock drops, then the investor gets to buy more shares for less money; if the price of stock goes up, the investor starts to make bigger and bigger profits.

As you can see, even small amounts of money can be invested for substantial profits. Next, as promised, I'm going to tell you about some people—people just like you—who used perspiration equity to leverage small amounts of money into large profits—and had a good time in the process.

Building Your Investments on a Solid Foundation

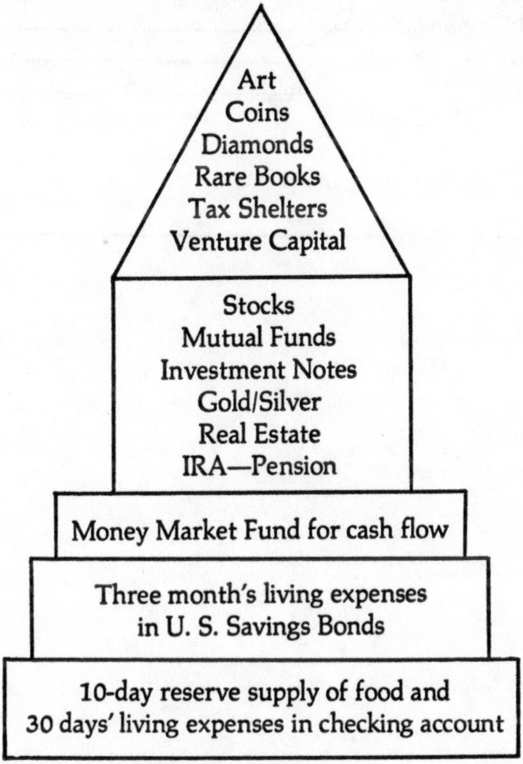

Art
Coins
Diamonds
Rare Books
Tax Shelters
Venture Capital

Stocks
Mutual Funds
Investment Notes
Gold/Silver
Real Estate
IRA—Pension

Money Market Fund for cash flow

Three month's living expenses
in U. S. Savings Bonds

10-day reserve supply of food and
30 days' living expenses in checking account

Your Tax Summary

Deductions, Withholdings and Estimates	Monthly Withholdings	Quarterly Estimates	Total Paid Annually
Federal Income Tax	$________	$________	$________
State and City Income Tax	________	________	________
Social Security Tax	________	________	________
Total Tax	$________	$________	$________

Chapter 10:
A Penny Saved

Coin collector Bill O'Neill of Davenport, Iowa, says that he became a rare coin investor rather by accident. Upon coming home from work each day, he tossed his loose pocket change into an open coffee can near the kitchen sink. A visiting relative asked him how long he had been doing that. Bill couldn't remember. It had been a habit of his for years.

The relative asked to see Bill's cans of coins. Upon examining them, he pointed out several things to Bill.

"For one thing, I had dozens of those black zinc pennies that were minted only in 1943," recalls Bill, "and they were worth about a nickel each. I had hundreds of the Lincoln pennies with the wheat stalks on the back, and they hadn't been made since the 1950s. Several were real finds. I also had buffalo nickels, liberty dimes, and Ben Franklin halves."

Bill bought a coin valuation book for $12.95 from a local coin shop and began to affix price values to his rarest coins. The noncollectible coins in his stockpile were put back into the coffee cans and were later spent to buy inexpensive cardboard coin albums.

"I discovered that the best way to market coins was by filling albums," says Bill. "In that manner, if buyers wanted my rare coins, they also had to purchase my less-valued coins. The purchaser wound up with a full display album, and I had a ready market for my total reserve of coins."

Bill subscribed to *Coin World* weekly newspaper and *Numismatic*

News magazine. The articles taught him how to appraise, price, and grade coins. The ads helped him find dealers eager to buy his extra coins, as well as collectors wanting to sell rolls, albums, or individual coins that Bill needed to enhance his collection.

"I joined two local coin clubs where some new friends showed me how to clean my coins, mount them in displays, and enter them in coin shows," says Bill. "It has been great fun. I've earned trophies, and my picture has appeared in several newspapers. I've made a lot more profit than I ever would have if I had simply put all that loose change into a bank savings account. Besides, I've had a marvelous time doing this."

Chapter 11: Profits from the Past

For Gene and Mary Kimpel of Fort Wayne, Indiana, collecting antiques in 1975 began as just a hobby. Today, that hobby has not only provided them with an impressively decorated home, but it also has helped them amass a collection of Early American artifacts worth thousands of dollars.

"Antique collections can be started with very little cash," Gene Kimpel says. "I advise people to check the attics and storerooms of their elderly relatives. What may be considered junk by one person may be a lost treasure to someone else. A relative of mine no longer wanted some handmade toys from the depression era. I knew someone who collected such items. I was able to trade that person those toys for two antique light fixtures that I needed for my collection. We both came out winners, but neither of us had to spend any money."

For beginners, Gene recommends reading *Antique Journal* for tips on collecting and evaluating antiques.

Gene also recommends going to farm liquidation auctions. Whereas most bidders will be there to get a good deal on a tractor or combine, antique hunters can frequently find quilts, cookware, picture frames, furniture, and books that have been handed down for several generations. They can be purchased inexpensively, cleaned up, and resold at a substantial profit.

"My wife and I enjoy browsing through flea markets, rummage sales, and antique shows," says Gene. "It's cheap entertainment. We haggle and dicker, find items to enhance our collection, and make some well-thought-out purchases. We've met some wonderful people and we've earned enough profit to put two sons through college."

Chapter 12: Know Book Value

Dick Weiderman of Grand Rapids, Michigan, began to collect books written by Jack London (1876-1916) because Weiderman was a fan of that author. His dream was eventually to have one copy of each of London's 58 titles. He put a want ad in his city paper seeking such books. More than 40 people called him.

"It was amazing," recalls Dick, smiling. "People had old books by Jack London in their basements, libraries, garages, attics—just everywhere. Some people gave them to me. Others looked at the original prices of the books ($1.75) and charged me that. A few people asked for big payments and I just said no and left."

For about $100, Dick wound up with nearly 350 varieties of Jack London books. Many were tattered, faded, or moldy. These he threw out. Some were cheap reprints that he kept as "trading" copies. Others, however, were first editions.

"I immediately fell in love with the first editions," says Dick. "The book paper was thick, the print was large, the page borders were wide, and the illustrations were gorgeous. I went to the library and checked the *Guide to Small Presses* and discovered there were three small-circulation quarterly journals being published about Jack London. I subscribed to all three. I also found a book called *Jack London First Editions* by James E. Sission III that helped me determine the value of my London books."

Dick was surprised to discover that some of the books he had purchased for a few dollars were worth from $50 to $75 or more.

He began to haunt used bookstores looking for more bargains.

"I discovered there was a Jack London bookstore in Glen Ellen, California," said Dick, "that would take my extra copies in trade toward editions I needed to purchase. This bartering helped me get rare titles at below-market prices."

Dick spent five years completing his collection (and reading it). One of his London books, *The Cruise of the Dazzler*, is valued at $4,500 because of its quality and scarcity. The total collection is valued at about $17,250. He spent roughly $3,800 putting it together.

"Along the way to completing my collection I also made several thousand dollars in profit," says Dick. "I bought an extra supply of London books during years when his popularity seemed to be waning. Then in 1976 the literary world celebrated the hundredth anniversary of London's birth. The subsequent publicity of that event drove up the value of London books, and I sold my extra copies at high profits to libraries, new collectors, and researchers."

Dick repeated that same procedure a decade later. After the hoopla over the hundredth anniversary died down, prices of London books drifted downward. Dick bought a good supply when prices were at their lowest (1979-1984). Then on January 11, 1986, the United States postal service issued a 25-cent Jack London commemorative stamp. The ensuing publicity increased the demand for London books and drove the price back up. Dick Weiderman again sold his supply of extra copies at a large profit.

"It's kind of like watching the stock market," says Dick, "except that London's novels are far more interesting to read than a company's business prospectus or quarterly report."

One of Weiderman's sideline ventures has been to take out-of-print books about Jack London (such as Martin Johnson's 1913 book *Through the South Seas with Jack London*) and to reprint them now that they are in the public domain. He has sold thousands of copies of these "lost" titles to libraries, collectors, and fans of Jack London. Though he has made about $27,000 profit since 1972 with his Wolf House Books reprint company, Dick says he is more pleased over the fact that his efforts kept these rare books from disappearing altogether.

Chapter 13:
Auto-matic Investments

Hal Souers of Warren, Indiana, is one of three thousand Americans who invest in Hudson automobiles for both long- and short-range profits. What makes Hal unique, however, is that he was only fifteen when he bought his first "junk heap" Hudson for $54 at an auction. Souers, by age 24, owned 84 Hudsons that he kept lined up in rows behind his parents' barn on a small farm. In 1986 he finished refurbishing a 1954 Hudson Hornet; his total cost for restoring the car was $1,200 and he sold it for $10,000.

"My grandfather owned a 1939 Hudson Terraplane," says Hal, "and I loved to ride in that big old car. I used to read books about the history of the Hudson Auto Company [1909-1956]. I studied auto mechanics in high school and used my summer farm salary to go to auto auctions to buy junked Hudsons. I would strip them of their parts until I had enough to put one complete car together. I then would sell it through an ad in the *Hudson Auto Collector's Newsletter* and use my profit to buy more cars. People kept telling me how impressive it was that I was making such large profits, but what they couldn't understand was how much fun I was having rebuilding those cars."

Souers says that when Nash Autos bought out Hudson in 1956, it discontinued its servicing of Hudson cars. When owners could not get spare parts, they flooded the used car market with Hudsons. Many of the cars were sold for scrap iron or were left to rust on vacant lots, in garages, or in barns. Today, they are a rare item again and Hal Souers finds them a very marketable product. He even has a large Hudson dealership sign on his family's barn and a flashing neon sign in his bedroom window.

"By mid-1987 I had five Hudsons that I had restored to mint condition, each with a market value from $11,000 to $20,000," says Hal. "I had nineteen other Hudsons that were adequately road worthy and sixty others in various degrees of disrepair that I used for spare parts. Interestingly, farming is still my prime occupation, but the profit I've made during my years in the Hudson restoration work has enabled me to build a five-car garage, as well as purchase two additional tracts of prime farm land. I don't know anything about the so-called sophisticated investments. Whenever anyone asks me if I've ever invested in the stock market, I say that I've made $80,000 in the stock car market. I invest in what I know something about."

Totaling Your Assets

Liquid:

Cash on hand (including checking account)	$________
Money Market Funds	________
Certificates of Deposit	________
Passbook Savings Account	________
Investment Notes	________
Life Insurance cash values	________
Mutual Funds	________
Total Liquid Assets	$________

Nonliquid:

Home and property (market value)	$________
Undeveloped property or farm land (market value)	________
Value of owned businesses	________
Rental properties	________
Limited partnerships	________
Boat, RV, motorcycle, trailers	________
Automobile(s) (market value)	________
Furniture, personal property, furs, jewelry (estimated market value)	________
Coin, stamp or rare book collections, antiques	________
Individual Retirement Account	________
Pension and profit sharing plans	________
Receivables from others	________
Total Non-liquid Assets	$________

Summary

These stories are but a few of the many true accounts of people who have used knowledge and work to transform a small investment into a large profit. Who knows—maybe in a future book I will be writing about you, and how you used your own perspiration equity to build your fortune.

The key things we discovered in this Part 3 were these points:

- The best time to begin an investment program is *now*.
- Even a small amount of money can be invested in many ways for a substantial return;
- By studying and learning all you can about a particular investment, you can develop a very enjoyable hobby while also making major financial gains.

Always remember, the way you handle money reflects on your life as a Christian. Be a good steward.

Part 4: Get the Most for Your Money

I remember once hearing a woman tell my wife, "It's not that we don't have enough money; it's just that we have too much month." We knew exactly what she was talking about.

When I was working on my doctoral degree, our family income was at the poverty level. I was earning $3,200 a year as a part-time college English teacher, and I was receiving $3,000 annually from the G.I. Bill of Rights as a veteran attending school. That equaled $516 per month. After we paid the rent, utilities, tithe, insurance, and taxes, we would have about $19.25 to spend on food, gasoline, tuition, and textbooks for the rest of the month. We, also, were faced with "too much month."

By necessity, we became experts at stretching a dollar. Even so, in order to get through, I had to take on a part-time job at the local newspaper, as well as take out a government-sponsored student loan. I learned to hate poverty. Despite what poets may tell you, people **cannot** "live on love." For groceries, heat, electricity, and clothing, you need cash.

It was at that time of my life I started a self-study program to learn all I could about money. My goal was not to become rich, but just not to be poor anymore. By studying about money I learned ways to reduce my taxes, enhance my earnings, and build my estate. Knowledge proved to be profitable. In this chapter, I want to share some basic dollar-stretching strategies with you, as well as encourage you to explore the myriad of avenues open to you for financial investments.

Most Christians know very little about the stewardship of investment. I recall that when the stock market crashed in October 1987, very few other Christians were as concerned about it as I was. It finally dawned on me that they weren't concerned because they didn't have any money invested in stocks. More to the point, they didn't have any money invested, period. (Even more to the point, some just didn't have any money at all.)

Like the unworthy steward who buried his talent in the sand rather than invest it, many of today's Christians are buried in the sands of debt and ignorance. Let's now explore ways in which we can become more like the men who pleased their master by properly increasing the value of their talents.

Chapter 14: Ways to Reduce Taxes

Because of the Tax Reform Act of 1986, most Americans now fall into either a 15 percent or 28 percent tax bracket. The 15 percent rate applies to joint filers with taxable income up to $29,750; the 28 percent rate applies to income above that level. Single persons pass into the 28 percent tax bracket after they earn more than $17,850. These are high taxes, despite the recent cutbacks.

New York's Justice Learned Hand once noted, "Anyone may so arrange his affairs that his taxes shall be as low as possible. He is not bound to choose the pattern which best pays the Treasury . . . nobody owes any public duty to pay more than the law demands."

Most people support such a concept, for nearly everyone hates to pay taxes. I now want to teach you some legal and ethical ways to reduce your tax burdens. Let me preface this, however, with an admonition that all taxes are not "hateful." Were it not for taxes, the city, state, and federal governments on which you rely for health care, police and fire protection, educational facilities, and other citizen benefits would not be able to function.

Sometimes we don't appreciate the work of tax dollars until the work stops. When California passed its Proposition 13 and rolled back state taxes, everyone was happy. That is, until six months later when potholes in the street weren't being fixed, state employees' raises were canceled, public libraries were closed, and state parks were left unmanaged. Tourism fell off dramatically, highway accidents increased, and property values dropped. Within a year the citizens were asking lawmakers for new taxes to pay for the services they had come to expect and enjoy. It would be a good thing for citizens of other states to remember this episode whenever they feel led to say, I wish I could avoid paying taxes altogether.

Remember this: **tax avoidance** is a strategy by which you do not have to pay more than the rightful amount of taxes you owe; **tax evasion** is an illegal maneuver used to try to avoid paying taxes at all. The former is wise stewardship; the latter is sin. Christ taught, "Render to Caesar the things that are Caesar's, and to God the things that are God's" (Luke 20:25). Trying to avoid appropriate taxes or appropriate tithes and offerings is wrong for a Christian. Paul emphasized this when he wrote, "Render therefore to all their dues: tribute [tax payments] to whom tribute is due; custom to whom custom [is due] (Romans 13:7).

My dad always used to say, "I would never complain about having to pay taxes on a million dollars." One day my brother Gary, an accountant, said, "Why not? You'd have to pay $385,000 to the government." My father smiled and said, "Just give me the million dollars and I'll show you just how content a man can be on a mere $615,000." His point was well taken. Perhaps we should dwell more on what we have rather than what we lack. That viewpoint will make it easier for you to pay your taxes.

Chapter 15:
Varieties of Income

Income can be divided into three basic types of income: taxable, tax-free, and tax-deferred. Your family accountant is the best person to consult about which of these avenues of income is of most importance to you. Knowing a little about each, however, can set you to thinking about financial options open to you.

Taxable income is the money you earn that is subject to immediate taxes. Your salary is a prime example. Taxes are usually withheld by your employer before you ever receive your paycheck.

Tax-free income is the money you earn or receive on which you do not have to pay tax. For example, you are allowed to receive up to $10,000 annually as an untaxed gift from a relative or benefactor. Another example is money earned on municipal bonds, since such earnings are totally exempt from federal income tax and sometimes from taxes in certain states, too. Certain inheritances are tax free. Also, a couple can now leave up to $1,200,000 tax free to heirs, or $600,000 if the surviving spouse owns all their property after the first one dies.

Tax-deferred income refers to earnings you are now accumulating on which you will pay taxes at a later time. For example, if you purchase a United States savings bond for $25, it will increase in value every year you hold it. You can either pay the tax on its annual earnings or wait and pay the tax on the profit you will earn after the bond reaches its maturity value of $50 and you redeem it.

Another example is an individual retirement account (IRA). The money put into an IRA will earn interest each year, but you do not have to pay tax on the earnings until you start to draw out the money after age 59½.

Numerous other legitimate tax shelters can be found—Keogh Retirement Plans, oil and gas exploration investments, equipment leasings, livestock ranches. You can look into these with the help of a certified financial planner or a trusted broker. For most people, however, a variety of more immediate pragmatic ways to use available cash can be employed, such as reducing the mortgage principle on your home.

One question that often arises when tax shelters are examined is, Can I limit my tax burden by channeling some of my money toward Christ-honoring organizations?" The answer is a resounding yes! Here's one example:

Most people know that the money they contribute to churches, missionary groups, and other charitable organizations is tax deductible if a person uses the IRS long form for itemized deduction listings. What is important to know, however, is that the donor can also have some control over the use of the money without losing the deduction. I could ask my church, for instance, to buy a $10,000 life insurance policy on me, listing the church as benefactor. I then could donate to the church the amount of money needed for the church to pay the annual premium (about $350). If I paid this for six years, the policy would then have enough cash value built up in it to pay its own premiums from then on. I would get a tax deduction each year that I donated the premiums ($350 per year X 6 years = $2,100) and when I eventually died, the church would receive $10,000 to assist its ministry. Thus, I could raise $10,000 for my church while simultaneously gaining $2,100 in tax deductions for myself.

Your insurance agent or church treasurer can help you explore a variety of other ways in which you can channel your tax-deductible dollars into organizations that are doing God's work. Religiously oriented colleges often have estate planners who can also help you in this area.

Chapter 16: Use Social Security

Although most wage earners complain continually about having Social Security payments withdrawn from their pay checks, statistically speaking it is one of the best investments most people ever make. If a woman retires at age sixty-five and lives to be eighty, she will draw from ten to twenty times more money out of Social Security than she ever paid in.

To make sure that your Social Security records are correct, you should compare your name and Social Security number with the name and number on your pay stubs during December and on the W-2 form you receive in January. The name and number should be identical on all these documents. The W-2 is the primary means of crediting earnings to your Social Security earnings record. Each year earnings are credited to records by matching the name and number on the W-2. Earnings are sometimes not credited because an incorrect name or number throws off the system.

The Social Security Administration is a computerized and highly automated organization headquartered in Baltimore, Maryland. Despite its technical equipment, it can make errors. Because of this, the SSA suggests that you run a check on your personal account every three to five years. (Errors discovered beyond five years are very difficult to correct.)

Checking is easy. Just obtain form SS-7004, "Request for Social Security Statement of Earnings," from any Social Security office. As you fill out the card, you can also write in, "Please furnish a benefit estimate," if you wish to be told what your monthly payment will be once you reach age 65.

Your statement will be sent to you in about one month. It will list your yearly total of credited earnings for the previous four years; all yearly amounts before that will be combined into one lump sum total. For the self-employed these totals can date back to 1951 and for wage earners as far back as 1937. (Earnings prior to 1937 do not count.)

Should you discover a mistake in your records, assemble your documents of proof and report all errors to your nearest Social Security office immediately. The most convincing documents that can be used to substantiate your argument are copies of your previous tax returns and the W-2 forms that show how much you paid in FICA taxes in specific years. Keep the government on its toes by double-checking all figures and records. It's your money: guard it.

Chapter 17:
Cover All Your Bases

A well-rounded plan for financial stability includes consideration of many factors. What if you become disabled? How will you plan for your estate? Challenge yourself to make faith pledges to insure the advancement of God's work on earth. While looking toward the future and saving, at the same time you will want to avoid excessively hoarding of the money you do have. This chapter will touch on each of these concerns.

Considering Disability

Approximately three out of every ten workers will become disabled either temporarily or permanently before even reaching retirement age. In effect, the odds are better than two-to-one you will never be injured badly enough to cause you to miss work for an extended period of time. Still, a loss of income even for a short time can be devastating for most families. Because of this, disability insurance coverage is worth considering.

You can use a mathematical formula to determine just how much disability insurance you really need to purchase. The base number is 70 percent of your current income. That's the amount of income that you will need to come in each month in order to maintain your current standard of living. (The reason it isn't 100 percent is because a person who is not able to work does not need money for daily travel expenses, union dues, packed lunches, and other expenses incurred on the job each day.)

So, multiply your current income by .70 to obtain your needed income during a disability. Subtract from that figure the amount of money you will receive apart from your salary (such as rents, stock dividends). The remaining figure is what you should insure yourself for.

Estate Planning

It used to be that the only people who gave thought to protecting their income and property through estate planning were those who lived on large "estates," with a mansion, servants, and several acres of land. Today, estate planning is appropriate even for apartment dwellers living on a fixed income.

In America, the average citizen is wealthier than 80 percent of the rest of the world's population. We accumulate furnishings, real estate, automobiles, insurance policies, jewelry, and a variety of other tangible assets. Upon retirement, we want these goods to serve us. Upon death, we want them to pass to the heirs of our choice. To guarantee this, an element of estate planning is necessary.

The first step is to have a will drawn up by your family attorney. This not only spells out your desires about the disbursement of your estate, but it also reduces the number of arguments among surviving heirs and prevents the state from stepping in and settling your estate for you. If you wish to establish trusts for loved ones or worthy institutions, you should designate how these trusts are to be funded, monitored, and administered.

Your next step is to analyze the capital (money value) of your estate. The "Estate Capital Analysis" form in this chapter will help you project your future cash needs by comparing your current income to your retirement goals. The "Objectives of Estate Planning" form will help you itemize the payments your estate will need to make upon your death in order to bury you, pay off the debts you leave behind, and award the bequests you have outlined in your will.

Faith Pledges

As Christians we should also be doing some estate planning for our home in glory. That, too, can be initiated now. By using the "Faith Pledge and Giving Plan" form found in this chapter, you can set giving goals for yourself each year. The amounts you select will be between you and the Lord, unless you wish to voluntarily make your pledge public as a way of showing your personal support for a particular Christian organization.

In setting your pledge goals, challenge yourself to contribute above your current means. Rely on prayer and your trust in God's bountiful blessings to help you reach your donation goals.

Avoid Excessive Hoarding

Whereas estate planning is wise for all people, it must not be taken to extremes. The Bible tells the story of a man who was so prosperous, he tore down his little barns and built bigger barns so that he could hoard greater amounts of wealth. When he died, however, the only thing that **counted** was the condition of his soul and his relationship to God.

Some people are innate hoarders. When family members went into the house of a relative who died a few years ago, they discovered that she had been hoarding clothes, food, money, blankets, dishes, medicines, and appliances for years. Her closets, spare rooms, basement, and garage were jammed with unopened store goods. It took five garage sales just to sell off items that could be carried by hand.

Everyone wondered what quirk could have been in this woman's personality to have made her feel the need to hoard so many objects. Psychologists such as Dr. Kathleen Gurney say that hoarding can be caused by a variety of factors. These include growing up during the Great Depression or having parents who were extremely thrifty or living in a family where you were always told there was never enough money or growing up in a neighborhood where you were known as the "poor kid."

Christian psychologists also add that many non-Christians who are hoarders are so aware of the vulnerability of their lost souls that they try to compensate by stockpiling tangible goods as protective reserves against any future bad times that may come.

A Christian who feels secure in his or her salvation knows that money can be used for better things than buying and hoarding material items that will never be used. An adequate savings is important; a secure soul is even more important. Any measures beyond that are subject to personal evaluation.

Income Tax Analysis

	Last Year	Estimated This Year
INCOME:		
Salary and Bonuses	______	______
Interest & Dividends	______	______
Business Income (Schedule C)	______	______
State Tax Refund	______	______
Schedule D Income	______	______
Schedule E Income	______	______
Other	______	
GROSS INCOME:	______	______
LESS ADJUSTMENTS TO INCOME:		
IRA/Keogh Plan	______	______
Business Cash Outlays	______	______
Married Couple Deduction	______	______
Other	______	______
TOTAL INCOME	______	______
LESS ITEMIZED DEDUCTIONS:	______	______
Medical Expenses (beyond 7½ percent of AGI)	______	______
Taxes	______	______
Interest on home mortgage/margin accounts	______	______
Contributions	______	______
Miscellaneous	______	______
Less Zero Bracket	(______)	(______)
TOTAL DEDUCTIONS	______	______

LESS EXEMPTIONS	______	______
TAXABLE INCOME	______	______
FEDERAL INCOME TAX	______	______
PLUS OTHER TAXES:		
Self-employment tax	______	______
Other	______	______
LESS CREDITS	(______)	(______)
TOTAL FEDERAL TAX	______	______
TOTAL STATE TAX	______	______
TOTAL TAX	______	______
MARGINAL TAX RATE	______	______
EFFECTIVE TAX RATE	______	______

Estate Capital Analysis

For

(Your Name)

19____	**Capital Requirements**	19____
$________	Immediate cash requirements	$________
$________	Additional cash requirements	$________
$________	Other cash requirements	$________
	Invested capital required at ____ percent net annual return to provide	
$________	____/month permanent income	
	____/month permanent income	$________
	Discounted capital required to provide	
$________	$____/month temporary income for years	
$________	$____/month temporary income for years	$________
$________	Capital required to produce other income	________
$________	Total Capital Requirements	$________
	Capital Assets	
$________	Cash	$________
	Stocks and bonds (net sale value—determine if these should be sold)	$________
	(Capital Gains Tax)	$________
$________	Life Insurance Net Estate Value	$________
$________	Subtotal Liquid Assets	$________
	Real Estate (net sale value—determine if these should be sold)	$________
	(Capital Gains Tax)	$________
$________	Death Benefit—Tax Qualified Retirement plan	$________
$________	Personal Property (net sale value)	$________
$________	Other Assets (net sale value)	$________
$________		________
$	ESTATE CAPITAL BALANCE	$
$________	Deficiency (-) or Surplus (+)	________

Objectives of Estate Planning

For

(Your Name)

IMMEDIATE CASH REQUIREMENTS	19___	19___
Funeral Expenses	$	$
Final Illness	$	$
Debt Retirement	$	$
Probate Costs ____%	$	$
Estate Taxes	$	$
Total	$	$
Additional Cash Requirements		
Emergency Fund	$	$
Mortgage Cancellation	$	$
College Funds	$	$
Total	$	$
INCOME REQUIREMENTS		
Permanent	$ /Month	$ /Month
Temporary (_____ Years)	$ /Month	$ /Month
OTHER CASH OR INCOME REQUIREMENTS		
Other Dependents	$	$
Charitable Bequests (such as church, school)	$	$
LEGAL DOCUMENTS		
Will		
Trust		

Faith Pledge and Giving Plan

I know that every good and great gift comes from God. As such, by God's grace and mercy, for the year ________ I pledge to give the following amounts of tithes and offerings to the noted ministries. Should I be blessed with unexpected additional income this year, I will increase these amounts accordingly. The amounts listed below will be a challenge for me to pay, but I will faithfully pray for God to provide the money for me to reach each goal.

Signed________________________

Dated ________________________

My tithe to my home church will be:	$________
My donations to widows and orphans and the poor will be:	________
My pledge for home missions is:	________
My pledge for overseas missions is:	________
My contribution to a Christian day school will be:	________
Grand Total	$________

Suggested Readings on Money Management

Ammer, Christine. *The A to Z of Investing.* New York: Mentor Books, 1986.

Bohigan, Valerie. *How to Make Your Home-Based Business Grow.* New York: Signet Books, 1984.

Brabec, Barbara. *Homemade Money.* White Hall, Virginia: Betterway Publications, Inc., 1984.

Curtin, Richard T. *Running Your Own Show: Mastering the Basics of Small Business.* New York: Mentor Executive Library, 1983.

Engel, Louis and Brendan Boyd. *How to Buy Stocks.* Boston: Little, Brown & Co., 1982.

Heatter, Justin. *The Small Investor's Guide to Large Profits in the Stock Market.* New York: Signet Books, 1983.

Hicks, Tyler G. *How to Borrow Your Way to a Great Fortune.* West Nyack: Parker Publishing Co., 1970.

Kishel, Gregory and Patricia. *How to Start, Run, and Stay in Business.* New York: John Wiley & Sons, 1981.

Mackevich, Gene and Sally S. Hodge. *Safe Low Risk Investments.*

Marcum, David and James B. Powell. *Ten Best Investments from $1,000 to $5,000.* Publications International, Ltd., Canada, 1986.

Marcum, David and Robert Meier. *Ten Best IRA Investments.* Publications International, Ltd., 1972.

Mattlin, Everett B. *How Much Are You Worth?* New York: Dreyfus Publications, Ltd., 1972.

Miller, L. D. *Best Rated Retirement Investments.* Publications International, Ltd., 1986.

Nessen, Robert L. *The Real Estate Book.* New York: Signet Books, 1983.

Orr, Lynn. *Government Guaranteed Investments.* Publications International, Ltd., Canada, 1985.

Stevens, Mark. *How to Pyramid Small Business Ventures.* West Nyack: Parker Publishing Co., 1981.

Van Caspel, Venita. *The Power of Money Dynamics.* New York: Simon and Schuster, 1983.

Weinstein, Grace W. *The Lifetime Book of Money Management.* New York: Plume Books, 1987.